Table of Contents

How to Use this Book

Pre-Writing Activities:

Read to your class - Each theme in this book contains a list of read-aloud selections. This is a wonderful way to enrich students' vocabulary and background information before they begin creating their own books.

Expand concept development - The instruction page for each theme contains suggestions for real items relating to the topic you can bring in to use for vocabulary and concept development.

Brainstorm - Brainstorming allows children with limited backgrounds to benefit, in a non-threatening way, from the experiences of their classmates. You may want to make a list of the words or ideas they share. Even children who are not yet reading can grow from this experience as it shows the relationship between what we say and the printed word.

Draw and/or Write a Story:

1. Blank Forms - Each child thinks about what his/her story will be. He/She then takes one or more forms, drawing an appropriate picture on each one. Many children will want to write something to go with their illustrations. (Young children will probably still be at the "invented spelling" level.) The finished pages are then stapled into the cover.

2. Blank Forms with Starter Sentences - Each theme contains three sentences containing empty lines for children to complete. Reproduce the blank page 3 times for your own use. Lay in one of the sentences on each of the three copies. Reproduce the copies for your students. Children complete the sentences in their own way and create appropriate illustrations. The three pages can be put together with the cover to create a simple book of their own.

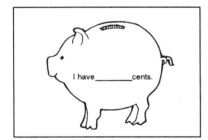  

3. Lined Form - Children write their story using as many lined forms as they need. The finished story is then put into a cover.

Putting Books Together:

Each child will need a copy of the cover and a blank sheet of paper. They lay the cover on the blank sheet, cutting out both a front and a back at the same time. Teachers may need to do this step for children with limited experience using scissors.

Other Uses for Cover Characters:

The reproducible pages in this book can be used in other ways.

Creating Class Books:

You can create class books of all types. Alphabet books, counting books, books about a specific phonetic element, books on a certain category of items, and simple nonfiction writings can all be created in a quick and easy way. Each theme gives you an example of a type of group or class book you can make.

You may want to make the covers of these class books out of card stock as they will probably get a lot of use in your class library. Thicker books can be put together using paper fasteners or laced up with yarn or a long shoelace.

Handwriting Practice:

Use the reproducible lined pages for handwriting practice. Children can practice single letters or whole sentences. They can also copy short poems using their "best" handwriting. If you have them copy or write their own poems, put the pages together to create individual or group poetry anthologies.

Cover Illustrations:

The cover pages can be used to decorate small bulletin boards.

They may be pasted to folders to create portfolios for childrens' work.

They may be used with the lined paper forms to create inexpensive journals for children to use.

Cookie Jar

Read

The Doorbell Rang by Patricia Hutchins;
  Greenwillow, 1986
If You Give a Mouse a Cookie by Laura
  Joffe Numeroff; Macmillan, 1976
The Roly Poly Cookie by Sara Murphey;
  Follett, 1964

Get Ready

1. Brainstorm to list all of the different
kinds of cookies.

2. Bring in a variety of cookies. Describe
them according to different criteria (shape,
color, size, contents, taste, etc.)

page 5

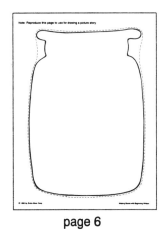

page 6

page 7

page 8

Make Individual Books
Prepare story forms and covers. (See page 2.)

1. Draw
Help children come up with their own topics for stories or use these.

My Favorite Cookies
Draw a different cookie on each form.

How to Make a Cookie
Draw pictures to show the steps.

2. Complete the Sentence
Child completes these sentences to create a three-page story.

I like _____ cookies best.
I drink _____ with my cookies.
Cookies taste _____.

3. Lines Form
Children write their own cookie stories. Possible story starters are...

Why I Like Cookies
Cookies in My Lunch Box
My Favorite Cookie
How to Make a Cookie

Make a Group Book
Reproduce the blank forms and the cookie forms.

Assign each child or pair of children a number. The
children color and cut out that number of cookies and
paste them on their form, then write or dictate
"I see (number) cookies in the cookie jar."

Staple all of the finished pages into a copy of the cover.
Place the book in your class library for everyone to enjoy.

Note: Reproduce this book cover for each child. Give them a blank sheet of paper to use to cut a back cover the same shape and size.

Cookie Jar Book Cover

Note: Reproduce this page to use for drawing a picture story.

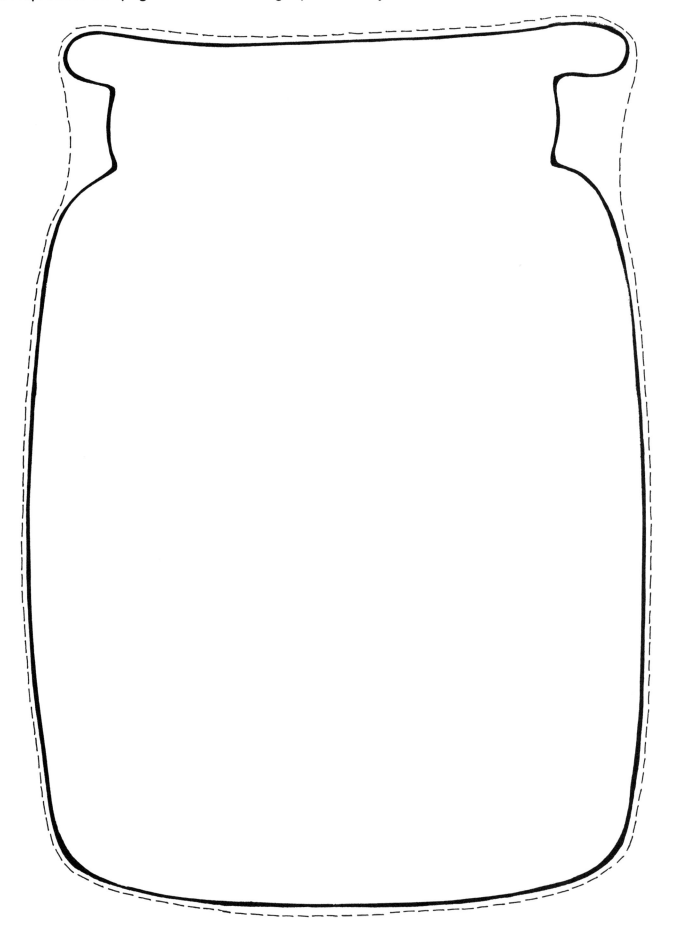

Note: Reproduce this page to use for written stories.

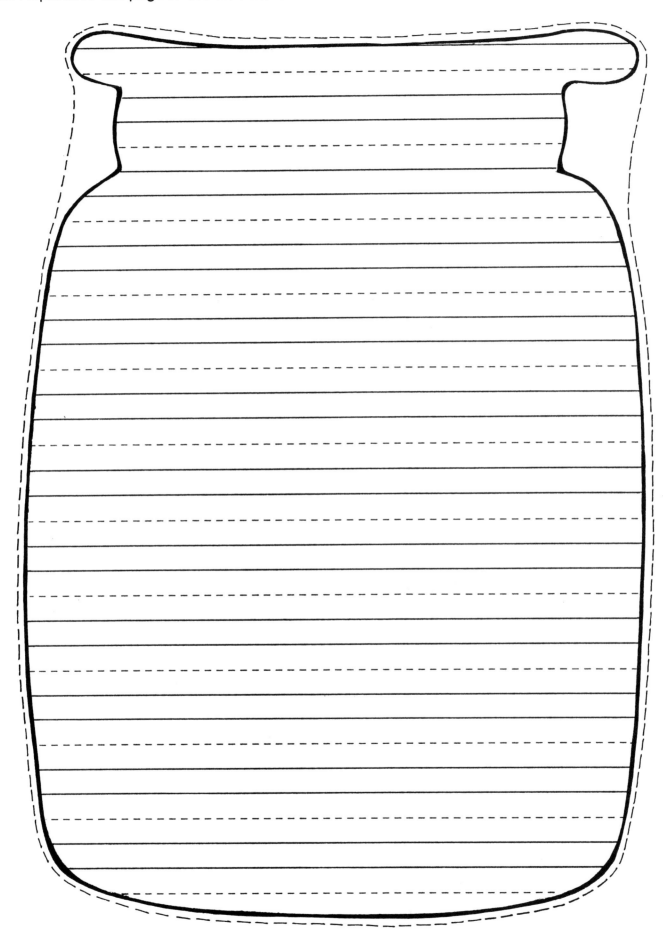

Note: There are directions on page 4 for using this page. The cookie shapes may also be used for practicing the hard sound /k/. Have children draw a picture on each cookie of something starting with the hard c sound.

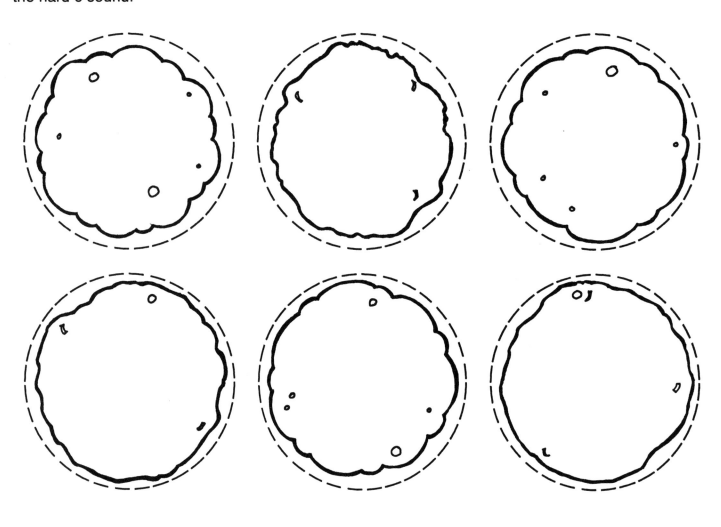

I like _____cookies best.

I drink _____with my cookies.

Cookies taste_____.

Making Books with Beginning Writers

Piggy Bank

Read

Alexander, who used to be Rich Last Sunday
 by Judith Viorst; Atheneum, 1978
Dollars and Cents for Harriet
 by Betsy Maestro; Crown, 1988
Piggy Bank Gonzales
 by Jack Kent; Parents, 1979

Get Ready

1. Bring in a collection of real banks and coins for your students to explore. Ask how many of them have a bank/save money.

2. Brainstorm all of the things they would like to buy. Talk about why we sometimes need to save our money before we can get what we would like. Discuss where they get the money they save.

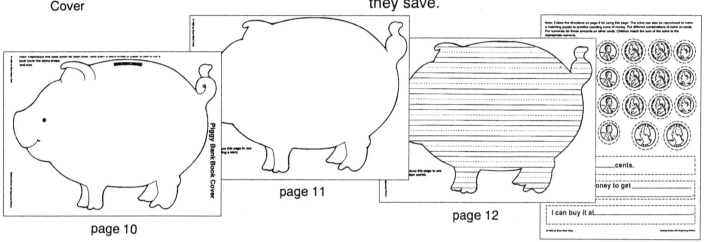

Cover

page 10

page 11

page 12

page13

Make Individual Books
Prepare story forms and covers. (See page 2.)

1. Draw	2. Complete the Sentence	3. Lines Form
Help children come up with their own topics for stories or use these. *If I Had a Dime* Draw an item you can buy if you have a dime on each page. *My Piggy Bank* Color the piggy bank shape	Child completes these sentences to create three-pagestory. I have _____ cents. I am saving money to get ———————————— I can buy it at a _(type of store)._	Children write their own piggy bank stories. Possible story starters are... At the Toy Store Inside My Piggy Bank How I Can Get Some Money My _(kind of bank)_ Bank

Make a Group Book
Reproduce the blank forms and the money forms.

Give each child copies of the blank pig form and the money form. They cut out and paste an amount of money on the pig form. Then they dictate or write, "I have _____ cents in my piggy bank." Staple all of the finished pages into a copy of the cover.

Piggy Bank Book Cover

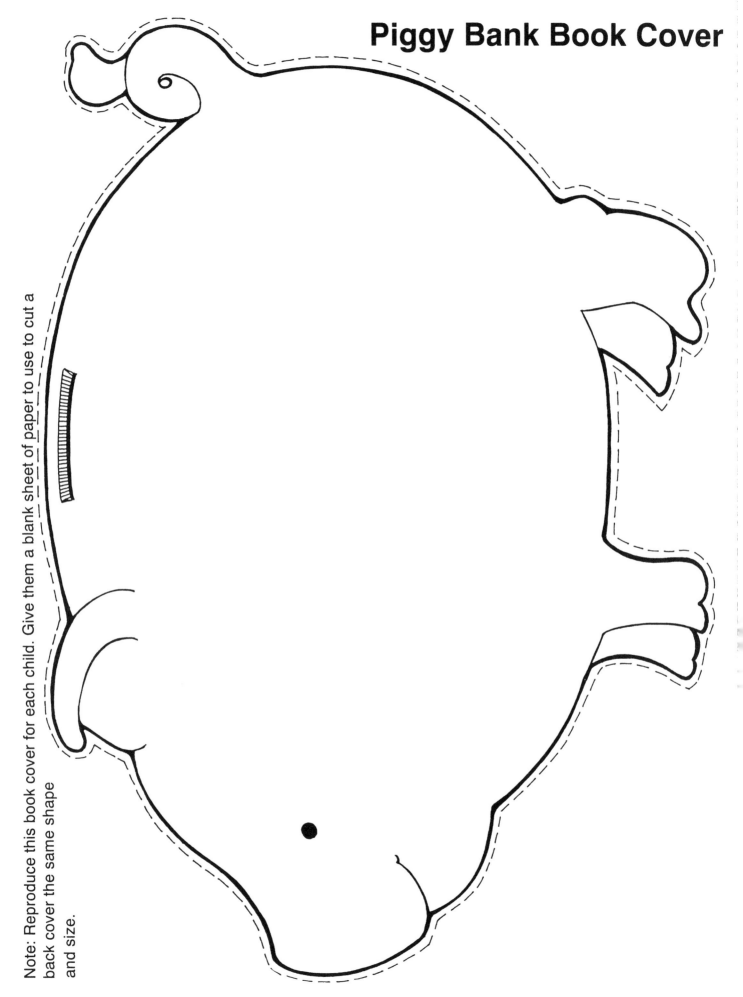

Note: Reproduce this book cover for each child. Give them a blank sheet of paper to use to cut a back cover the same shape and size.

Making Books with Beginning Writers

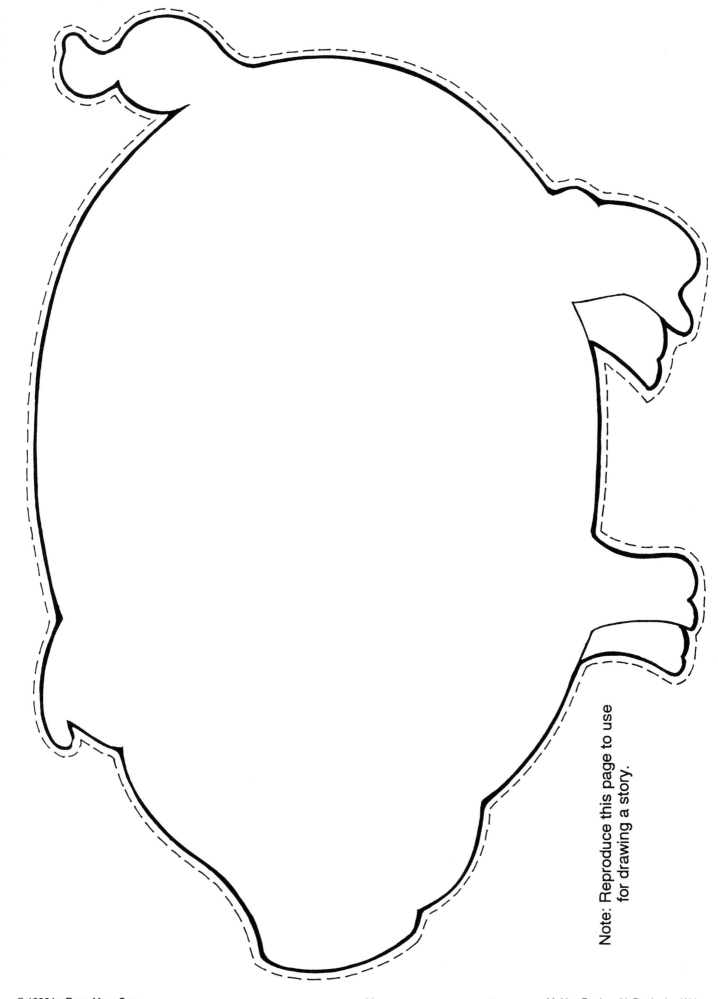

Note: Reproduce this page to use for drawing a story.

11

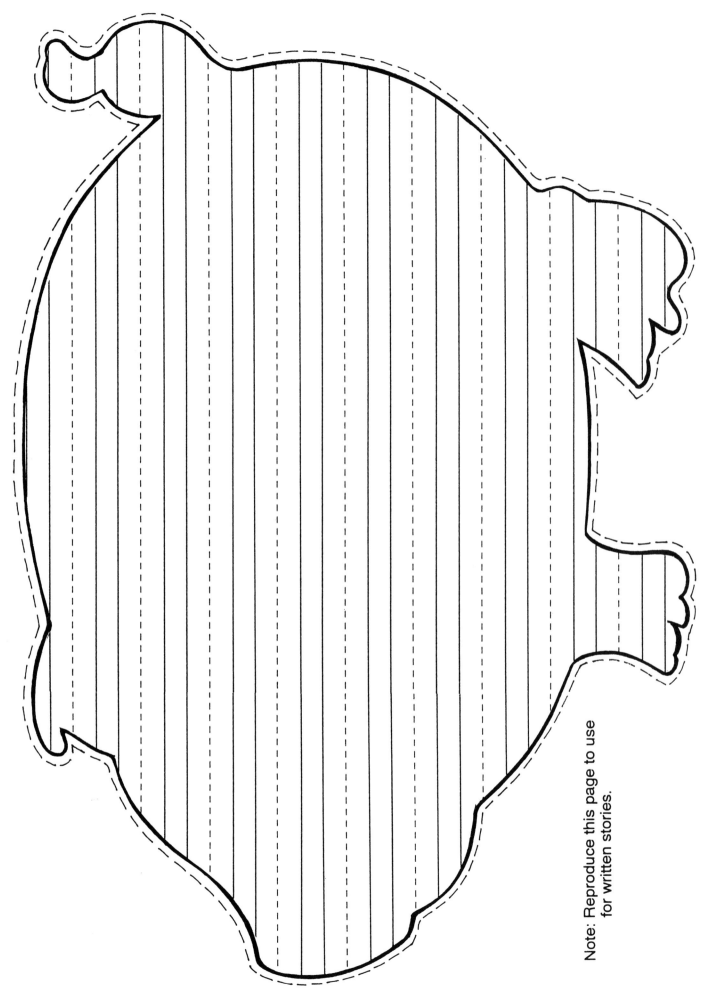

Note: Reproduce this page to use for written stories.

Note: Follow the directions on page 9 for using this page. The coins can also be reproduced to make a matching puzzle to practice counting sums of money. Put different combinations of coins on cards. Put numerals for those amounts on other cards. Children match the sum of the coins to the appropriate numeral.

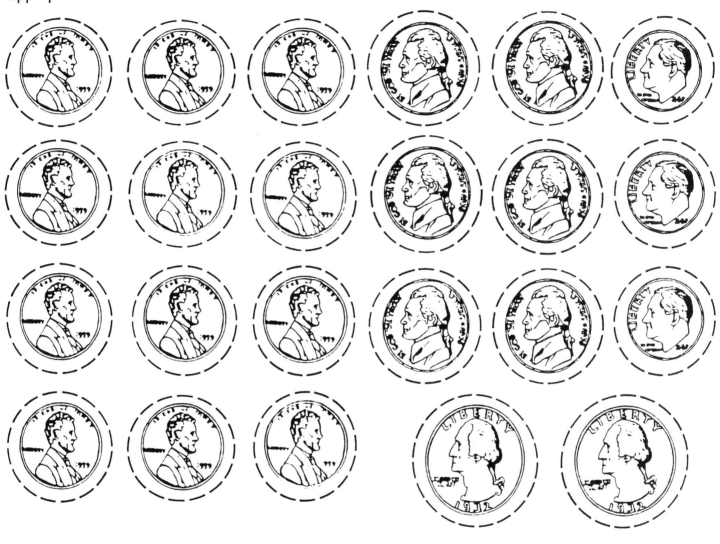

I have _____ cents.

I am saving money to get _____

_____.

I can buy it at_____.

DOG HOUSE

Read

Spot Goes to school by Eric Hill;
Putnam's, 1984
A Bag of Puppies by Dick Gackenbach;
Houghton, 1981
Daniel's Dog by Jo Ellen Bogart;
Scholastic Inc., 1990

Get Ready

1. Brainstorm to name all of the kinds of dogs. and magazines.

2. Discuss students' own dogs. What kinds do they have, what do the dogs look like, what can the dogs do, how they take care of their dogs, etc.

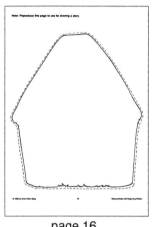

page 15
page 16
page 17
page 18

Make Individual Books
Prepare story forms and covers. (See page 2.)

| **1. Draw**
Help children come up with their own topics for stories or use these.

My Dog Can Do Tricks
Child draws his/her dog doing various types of tricks.

I Take Care of My Dog
Child draws self caring for and playing with his/her dog. | **2. Complete the Sentence**
Child completes these sentences to create a three-page story.

See my _____, ____ dog.
My dog can _____.
I take good care of my dog.
I _____. | **3. Lines Forms**
Children write their own dog stories. Possible story starters are...

How to Give a Dog a Bath
My Pet Dog
Dog Tricks
The Best Dog in the World |

Make a Group Book
Reproduce the blank forms and the cookie forms.

Give each child a blank form and one dog bone. They are to draw a dog and a dog dish inside the dog house. Then write the name of the dog on the dish and put one or more bones in the dish. Children who are ready to write may want to add a sentence or two about their dog. Staple all of the finished pages into the cover.

Note: Reproduce this book cover for each child. Give them a blank sheet of paper to use to cut a back cover the same shape and size.

Dog House Book Cover

Note: Reproduce this page to use for drawing a story.

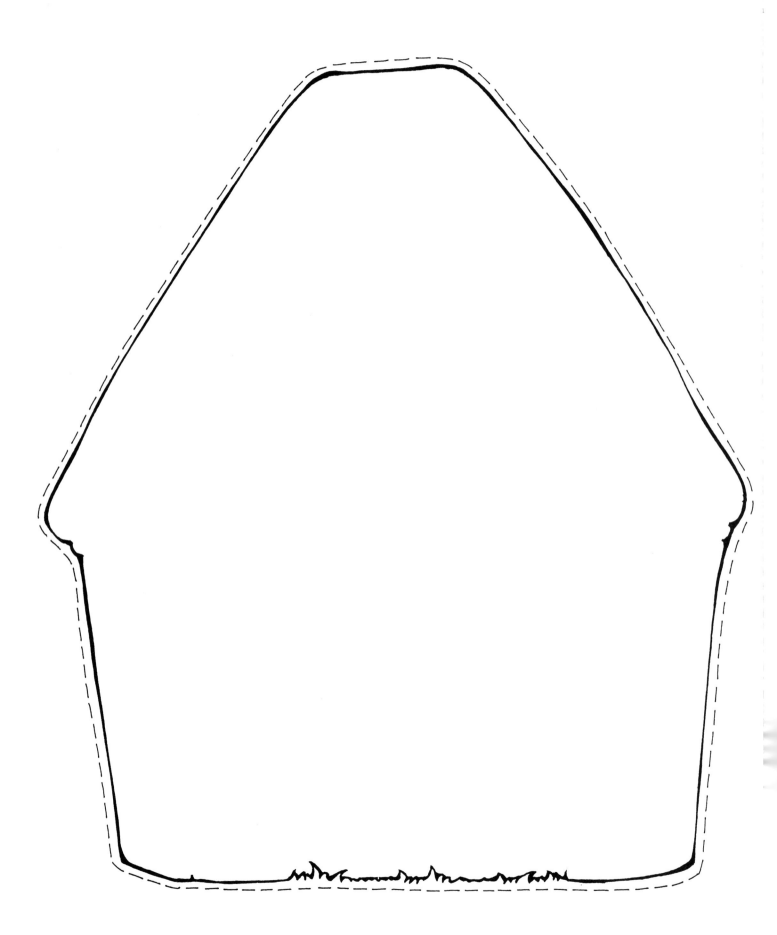

Note: Reproduce this page to use for written stories.

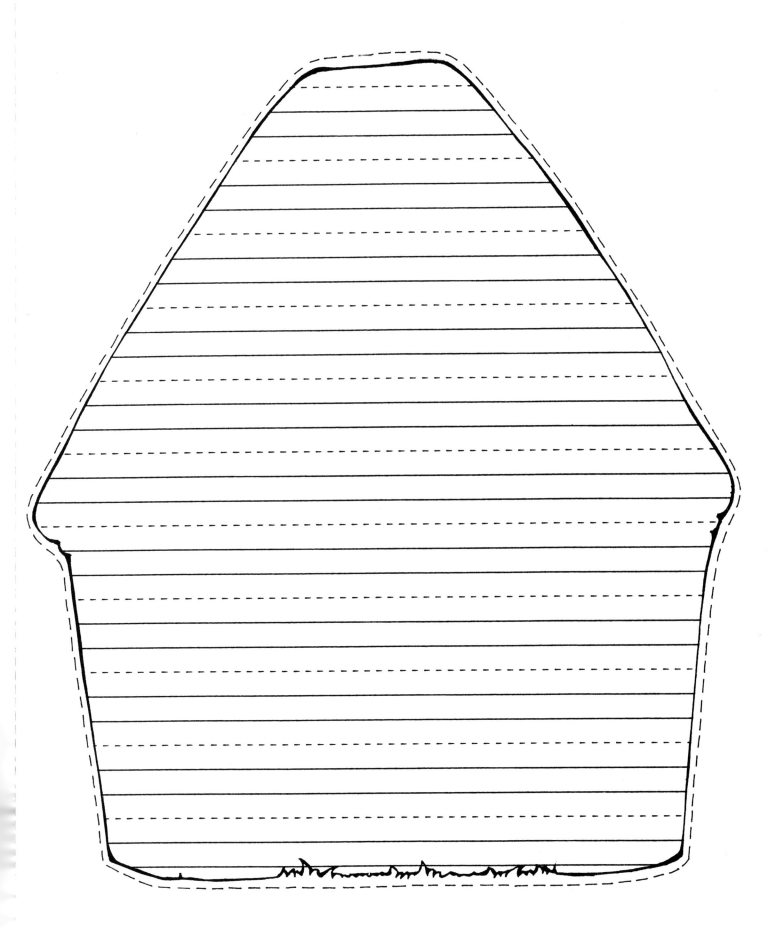

Note: Follow the directions on page 14 for using this page. The bones can also be used for counting practice. Reproduce a quantity of the bones. Bring in small dishes to be dog food dishes. Write a numeral on each dish. Children count the correct number of bones into each dish.

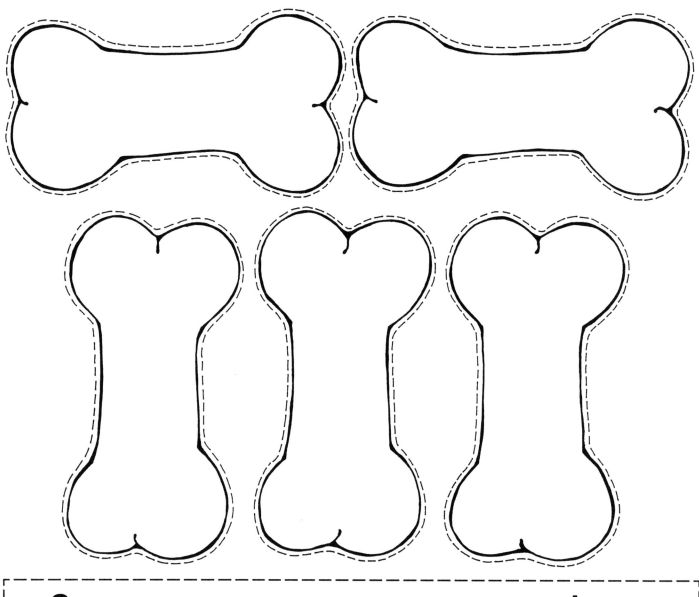

See my _____, _____ dog.

My dog can _____.

I take good care of my dog.
I _____.

Lunch Box

Read

Lunch Boxes by Fred Ehrlich;
Penguin, 1991
Jackie's Lunch Box by Anna Grossnickle Hines;
Greenwillow, 1991
What a Good Lunch by Watanabe;
Philomel, 1991

Get Ready

1. Have children show the type of lunch box or bag they bring to school. Bring in other types that they might not have seen before.

2. Brainstorm to list all of the kinds of food you might pack in your lunch box or bag. Discuss the kinds of covers, wrappings, or containers these items might need. See if they can come up with foods that would never be packed in a lunch box and explain why.

page 20

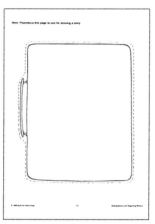

page 21

page 22

page 23

Make Individual Books
Prepare story forms and covers. (See page 2.)

1. Draw	2. Complete the Sentence	3. Lines Form
Help children come up with their own topics for stories or use these. How to Make a Sandwich Draw pictures to show the steps. _(child's name) 's_ Lunch Child draws a different item he/she would like for lunch on each page (sandwich, fruit, cookie, drink, etc.).	Child completes these sentences to create a three-page story. My lunch box is ————— I have —————————— for lunch today. I wish I had ——————————	Children write their own lunch box stories. Possible story starters are... How to Make a Sandwich My Favorite Lunch A Surprise in My Lunch Box The Awful Lunch

Make a Group Book

Reproduce the blank forms and the food forms.
Talk about real and unusual sandwiches. Give each child a blank form and the bread form on page 23. He/She colors and cuts out the bread, create a surprise sandwich. Paste the sandwich to the lunch box form. Then write or dictate the ingredients. Staple all of the pages into a cover.

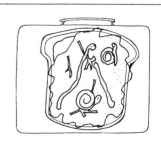

Making Books with Beginning Writers

Note: Reproduce this book cover for each child. Give them a blank sheet of paper to use to cut a back cover the same shape and size.

Lunch Box Book Cover

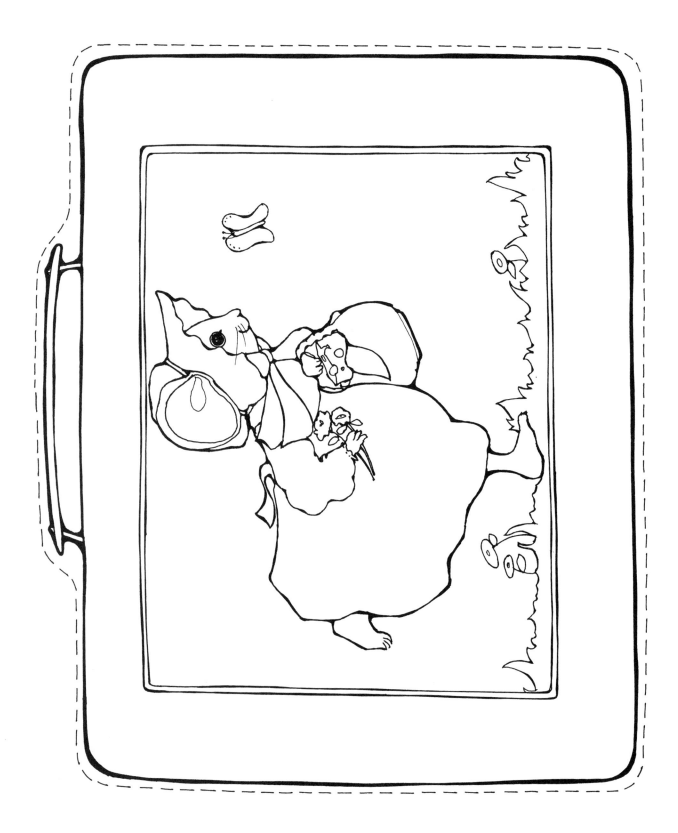

Making Books with Beginning Writers

Note: Reproduce this page to use for drawing a story.

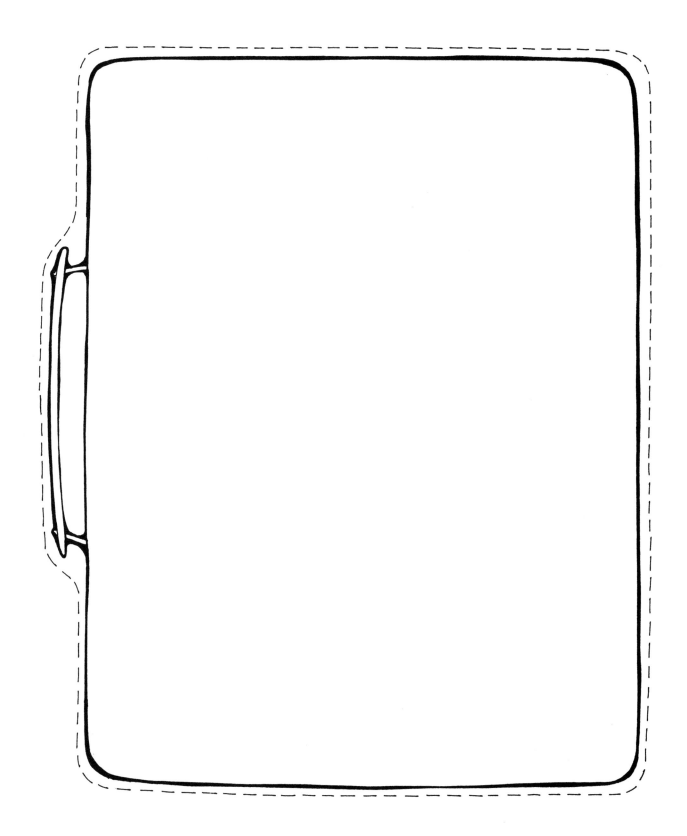

 Making Books with Beginning Writers

Note: Reproduce this page to use for written stories.

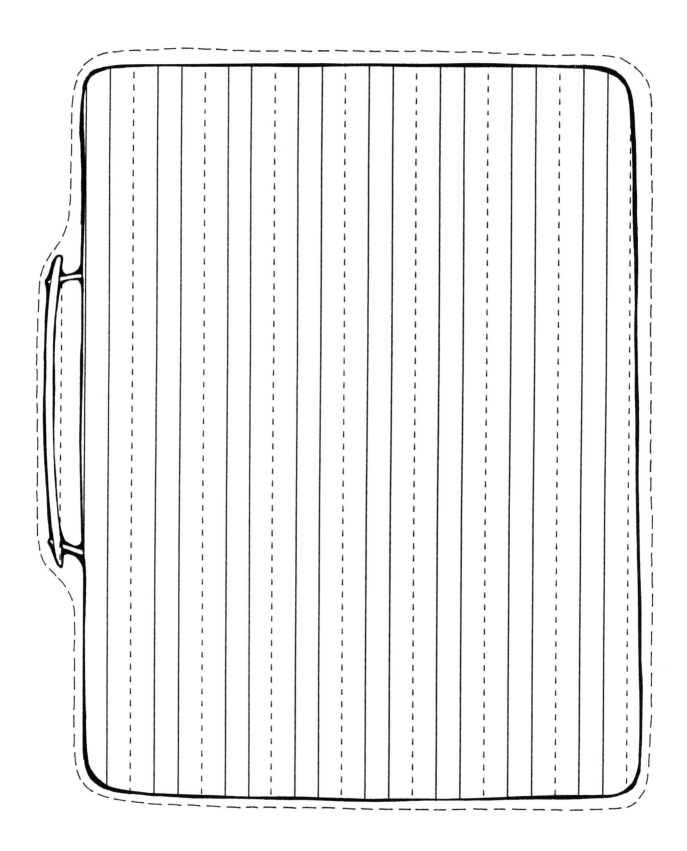

Note: Follow the directions on page 19 for using this page. The bread slice forms can also be used for patterning. Run some on white paper and some on brown paper. Give each child several copies of each. Have your students copy patterns you demonstrate. Start easy, increasing difficulty as the children experience success.

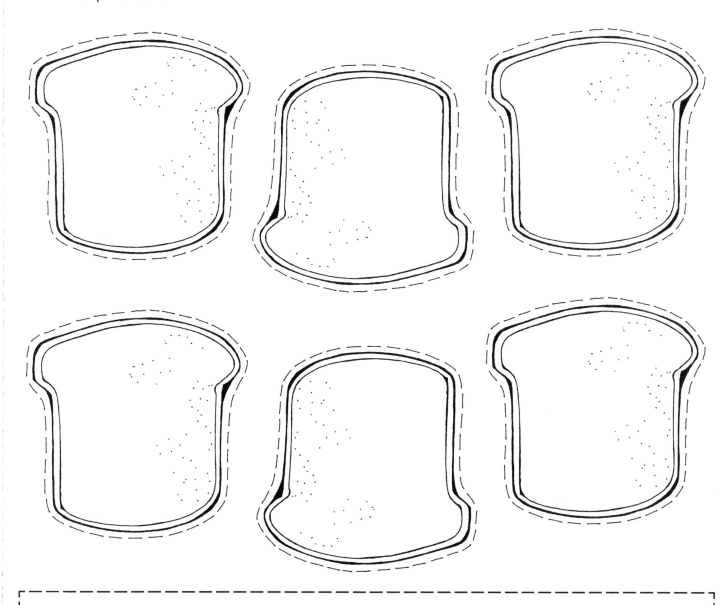

My lunch box is _____ .

I have _____ for lunch today.

I wish I had _____ .

Pocket

Read

Katy No Pocket by Emmy Payne;
Houghton, 1944

Peter's Pocket by Judy Barrett;
Antheneum, 1974

A Pocket for Corduroy by Don Freeman
Viking, 1978

Get Ready

1. Examine pockets on your students' clothing to discuss shape, number each is wearing, etc. You may even want to create a class graph of pockets.

2. Have children empty their pockets. Make a list of all the items they are carrying. (Allow children to decline if they don't want to share with the class.) Have your students think of unusual things they

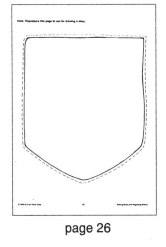

page 25

page 26

page 27

page 28

Make Individual Books

Prepare story forms and covers. (See page 2.)

1. Draw	2. Complete the Sentence	3. Lines Form
Help children come up with their own topics for stories or use these.	Child completes these sentences to create a three-page story.	Children write their own pocket stories. Possible story starters are...
In My Pocket Child draws a different item in each pocket form.	I have two pockets in my	A Hole in My Pocket In a Circus Clown's Pocket
All Kinds of Pockets Child draws a different type of pocket on each page (in jeans, in a jacket, on a kangaroo, etc.)	I keep _____ in my big pocket. I keep _____ in my small pocket.	No Pockets My Secret Pocket

Make a Group Book

Reproduce blank forms, lined forms and the objects from page 28.

Children get a blank form and a lined form. They draw something on the blank form or choose something from the object forms to paste to the pocket. Then write a short riddle about the object on the lined form. Staple all of the riddles and answers in a cover, being sure that the riddle page is on top of the answer page each time.

Note: Reproduce this book cover for each child. Give them a blank sheet of paper to use to cut a back cover the same shape and size.

Pocket Book Cover

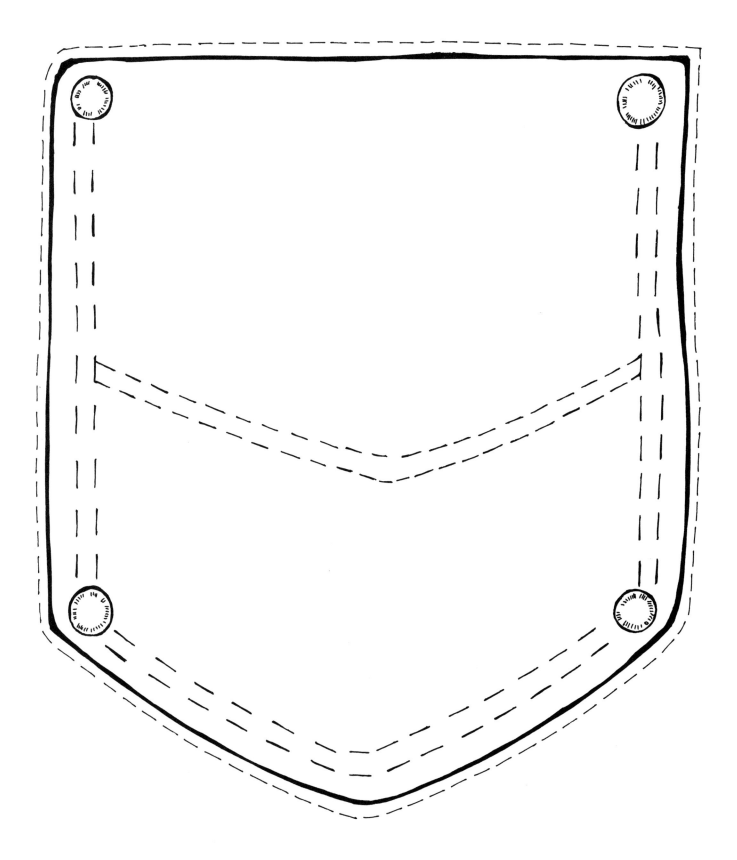

Note: Reproduce this page to use for drawing a story.

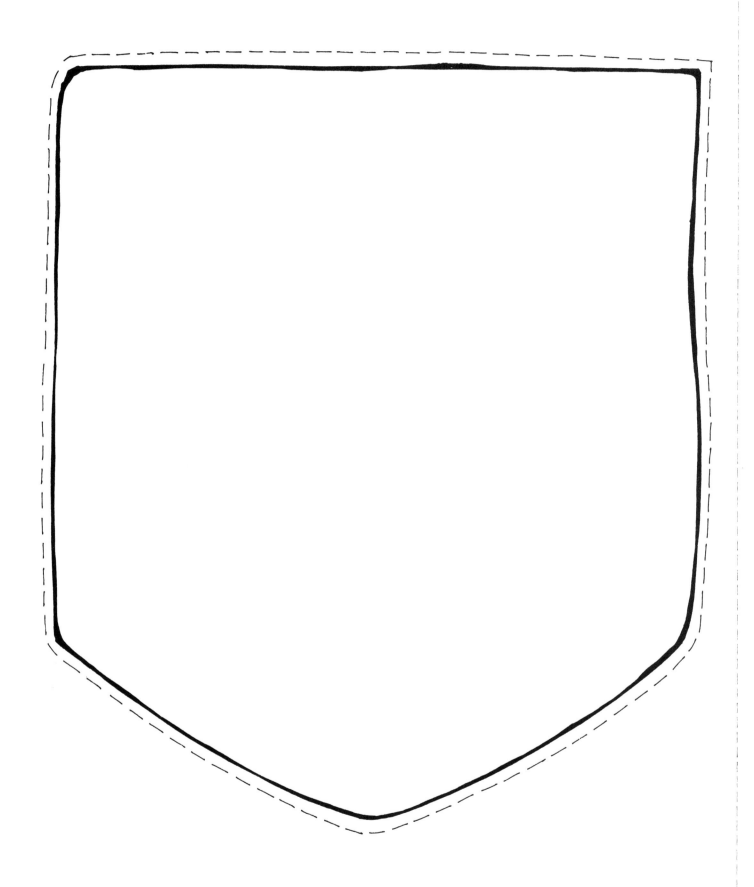

 Making Books with Beginning Writers

Note: Reproduce this page to use for written stories.

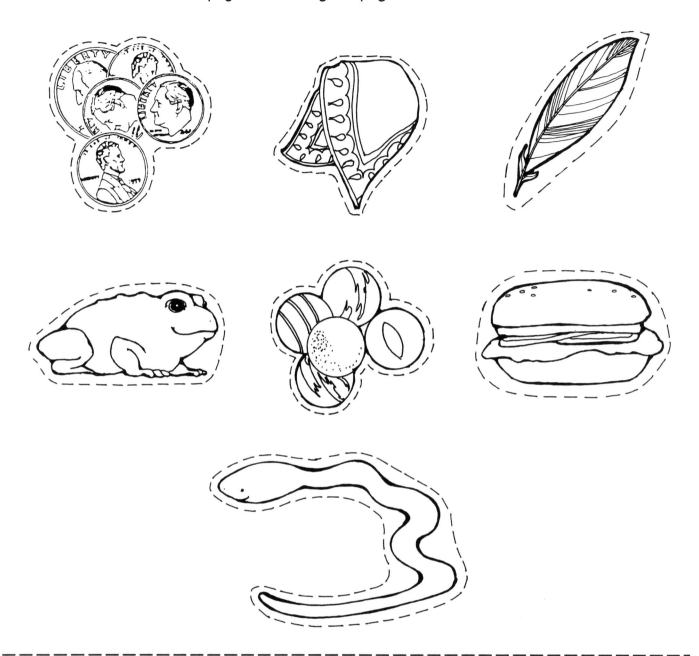

I have two pockets in my _____.

I keep _____
in my big pocket.

I keep _____
in my small pocket.

Fish Bowl

Read

Brian Wildsmith's Fishes by Brian Wildsmith;
Watts, 1968

Fish Eye by Lois Ehlert;
Harcourt, 1990

One Fish, Two Fish, Red Fish, Blue Fish
by Dr. Seuss; Random, 1960

Get Ready

1. Set up a fish bowl in the classroom. Include a couple of fish, some rocks or sand, small plants, and a water snail. Use the fish bowl to develop vocabulary and to help children understand how to take care of pet fish.

2. Collect pictures of different types of fish. Use these pictures for comparing and contrasting. This is also an excellent way to increase vocabulary.

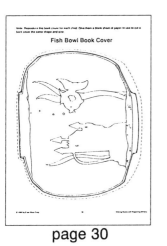
page 30

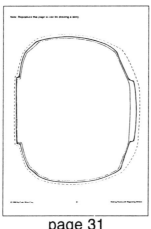
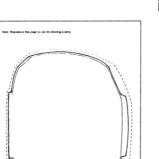
page 31

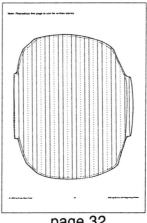
page 32

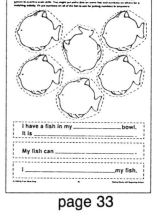
page 33

Make Individual Books
Prepare story forms and covers. (See page 2.)

1. Draw
Help children come up with their own topics for stories or use these.

Colorful Fish
Child draws a fish on each page using a different color and pattern. Write the word for the color used on the page.

My Pet Fish
Child draws a picture on each page showing how to take care of a pet fish.

2. Complete the Sentence
Child completes these sentences to create a three-page story.

I have a fish in my bowl.
It is _____.
My fish can _____.
I _____ my fish.

3. Lines Form
Children write their own fish stories. Possible story starters are...

Pet Fish
Strange Fish in My Bowl
A Birthday Surprise

Make a Group Book
Reproduce the blank forms and the fish forms.

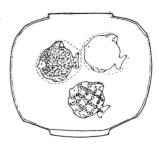

You will need a box of 24 or 48 crayons for this activity
Give each child a copy of the blank form, three fish and a crayon.
Each child is to use a different color for his/her page in the Rainbow Book. They are to make one fish dark, one fish light, and one fish with a pattern of light and dark using only the one color they have been given. Write the color at the bottom of the page and staple all of the fish bowls into a cover.

 Making Books with Beginning Writers

Note: Reproduce this book cover for each child. Give them a blank sheet of paper to use to cut a back cover the same shape and size.

Fish Bowl Book Cover

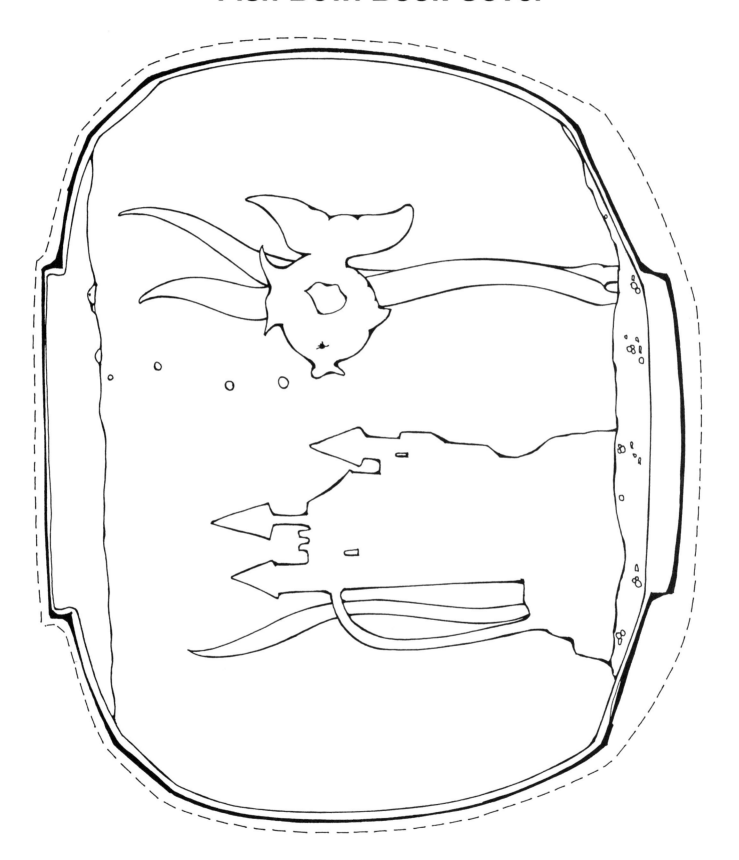

 Making Books with Beginning Writers

Note: Reproduce this page to use for drawing a story.

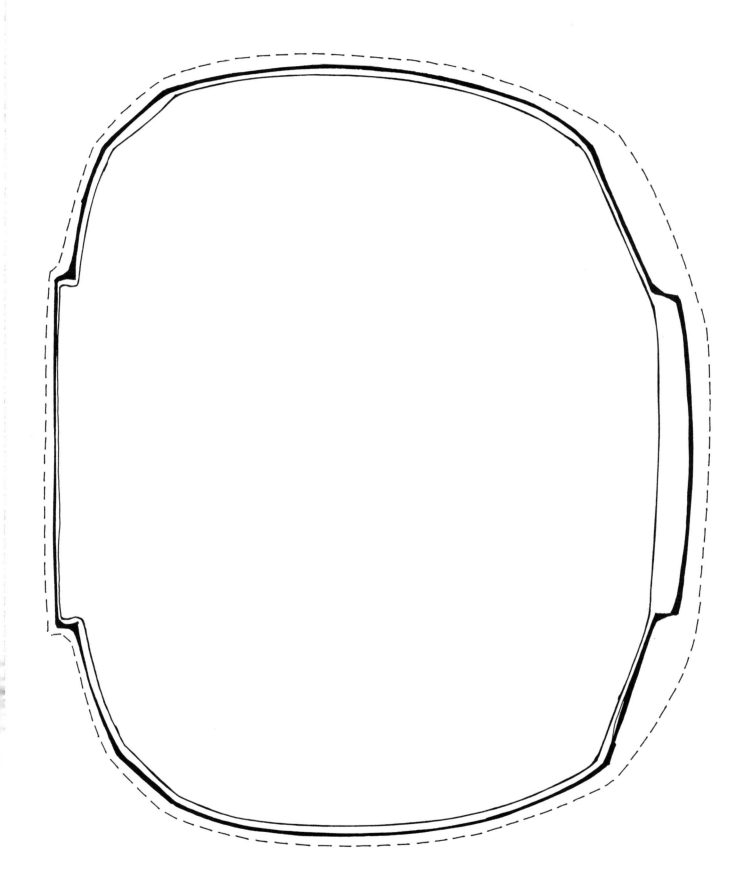

31

Note: Reproduce this page to use for written stories.

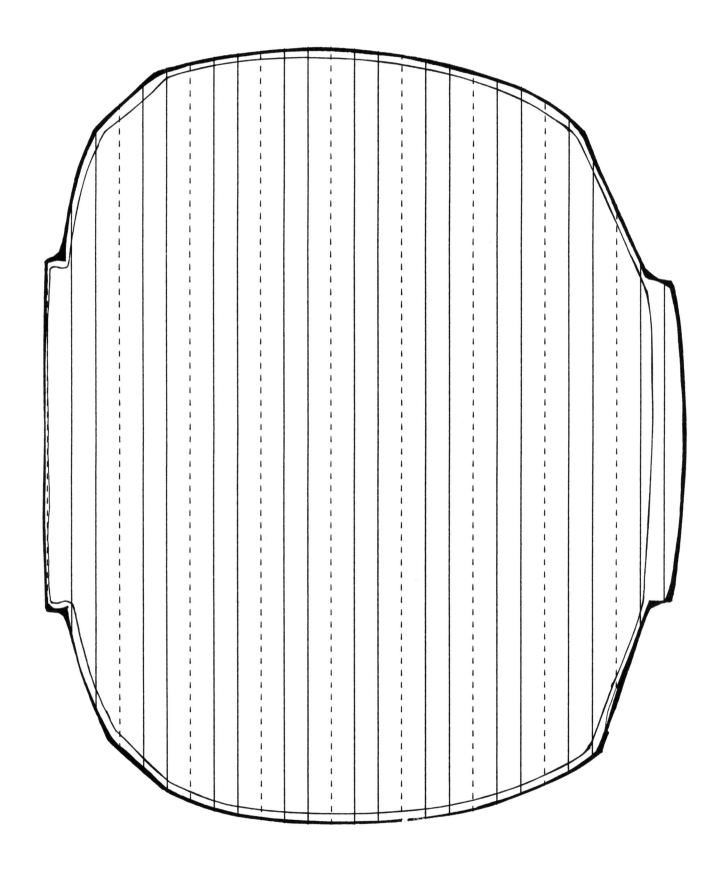

Note: Follow the directions on page 29 for using this page. The fish can also be used to create games to practice math skills. You might put polka dots on some fish and numbers on others for a matching activity. Or put numbers on all of the fish to use for putting numbers in sequence.

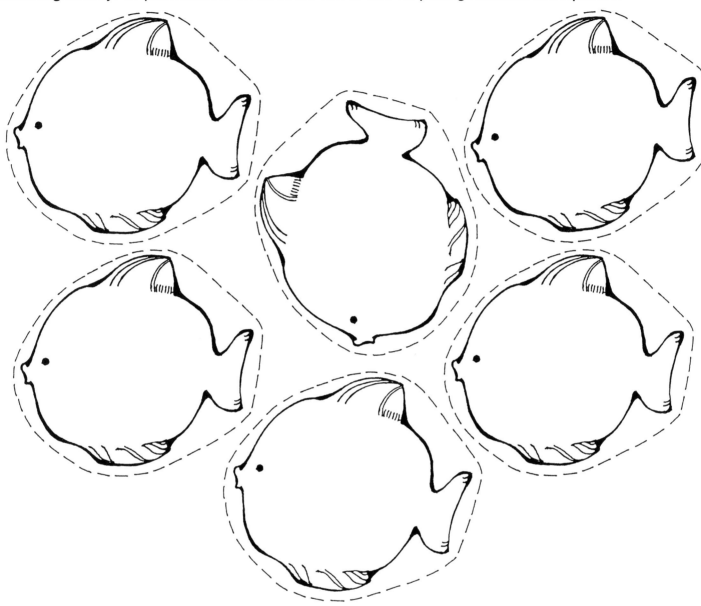

I have a fish in my _____ bowl.
It is _____ .

My fish can _____ .

I _____ my fish.

Circus Tent

Read

Babar's Little Circus Star by Laurent de Brunhoff; Random, 1988

Spot Goes to the Circus by Eric Hill; Putnam's, 1989

Curious George Rides a Bike by H. A. Rey; Houghton, 1952

Get Ready

1. Discuss what objects, animals and people you find in a circus. Talk about the costumes they wear and what kinds of acts the animals and people do.

2. Guide children to act out different circus animal movements and sounds (elephant, tigers, horses) and the actions of different people in the circus (acrobat, clown, juggler, etc.).

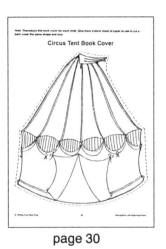

page 30

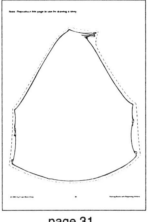

page 31

page 32

page 33

Make Individual Books

Prepare story forms and covers. (See page 2.)

1. Draw

Help children come up with their own topics for stories or use these.

People in the Circus
Child draws a different circus performer on each page.

A Trip to the Circus
Child draws a different scene on each page showing his/her family's trip to the circus.

2. Complete the Sentence

Child completes these sentences to create a three-page story.

I went to the circus with

_____

I saw a clown

_____

I saw a

_____

3. Lines Form

Children write their own circus stories. Possible story starters are...

Funny Clowns
The Lion Tamer
Elephant Tricks
Under the Big Tent

Make a Group Book

Reproduce the blank forms, lined forms and the patterns on page 38.

Give each child a blank form and a copy of the clown, circus dog, and ball. They color, cut out and paste the three pictures to the blank page. Then write or dictate these sentences using positional words. ("The funny puppy is behind my clown. The red ball is over the clown's head.") Staple the pages together in a cover.

Note: Reproduce this book cover for each child. Give them a blank sheet of paper to use to cut a back cover the same shape and size.

Circus Tent Book Cover

Making Books with Beginning Writers

Note: Reproduce this page to use for drawing a story.

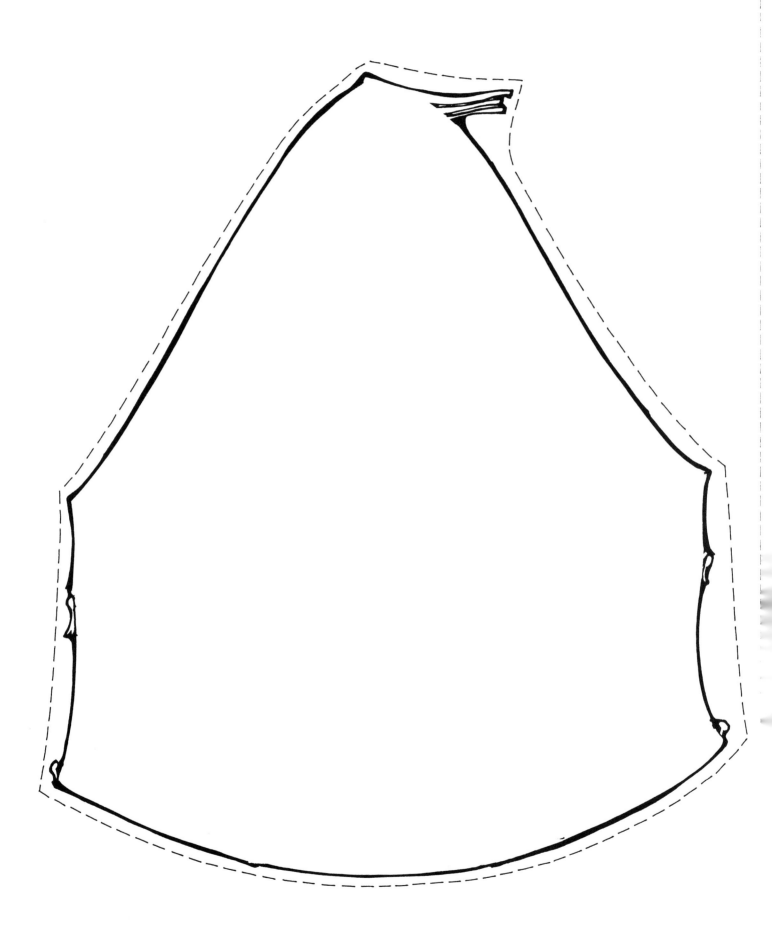

Note: Reproduce this page to use for written stories.

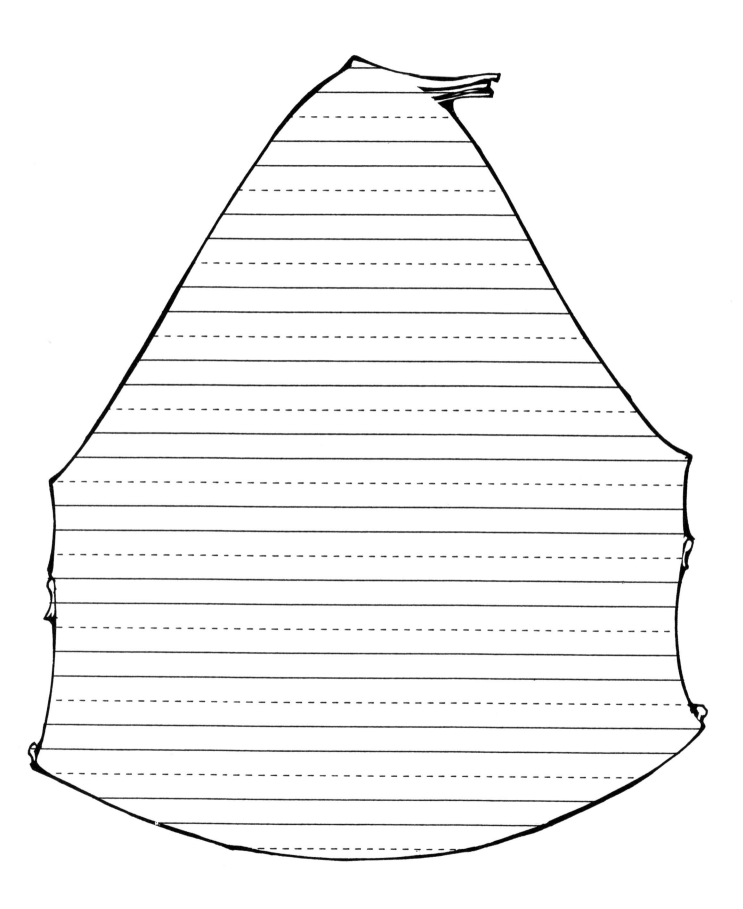

Note: Follow the directions on page 34 for using this page. Children may use the clowns and balls to create simple counting books by pasting a clown on a page, writing a number in the corner of the page and pasting the correct number of balls by the clown.

I went to the circus with _____.

I saw a clown _____.

I saw a _____.

Duck

Read

The Story about Ping by Marjorie Flack;
Viking, 1933
Across the Stream by Mirra Ginsburg;
Greenwillow, 1982
A Duckling is Born by Hans-Heinrich Isenbart;
Putnam's, 1981

Get Ready

1. Brainstorm to find out all your children know about ducks. What do they look like? Where do they live? What can they do?
2. Baby ducks are called ducklings. Discuss other birds and what their babies are called. You may want to extend the discussion to other types of animals and what their babies are called.

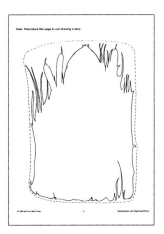

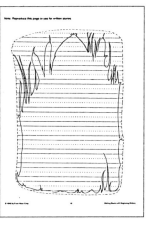

| page 40 | page 41 | page 42 | page 43 |

Make Individual Books
Prepare story forms and covers. (See page 2.)

1. Draw	2. Complete the Sentence	3. Lines Form
Help children come up with their own topics for stories or use these. Ducklings Give each child three duckling patterns. They paste one on each page and tell what it is doing. On the Farm Child draws a story showing a duck living on a farm.	Child completes these sentences to create a three-page story. See the big duck. She is __(where?)__ . She is __(doing what?)__ . Her ducklings are __(doing what?)__ .	Children write their own duck stories. Possible story starters are... Ducks at the Pond Ducks on a Farm Mother Duck and Her Ducklings Little Yellow Ducklings

Make a Group Book
Reproduce the blank form and the ducklings on page 43.

Give each child a blank form and a duckling. Children color and cut out the duckling, paste it to the form, then draw something beginning with the /d/ sound on the page. Finally have children dictate or write a phrase naming what is on the page ("a duck in a dish," "a duck eating doughnuts"). Staple the pages in a cover.

You might also use the duck and duckling theme to make a book of animal mothers and babies. Each child draws a mother and her baby, and dictates or writes what each is called (ewe, lamb).

Note: Reproduce this book cover for each child. Give them a blank sheet of paper to use to cut a back cover the same shape and size.

Duck Book Cover

Note: Reproduce this page to use for drawing a story.

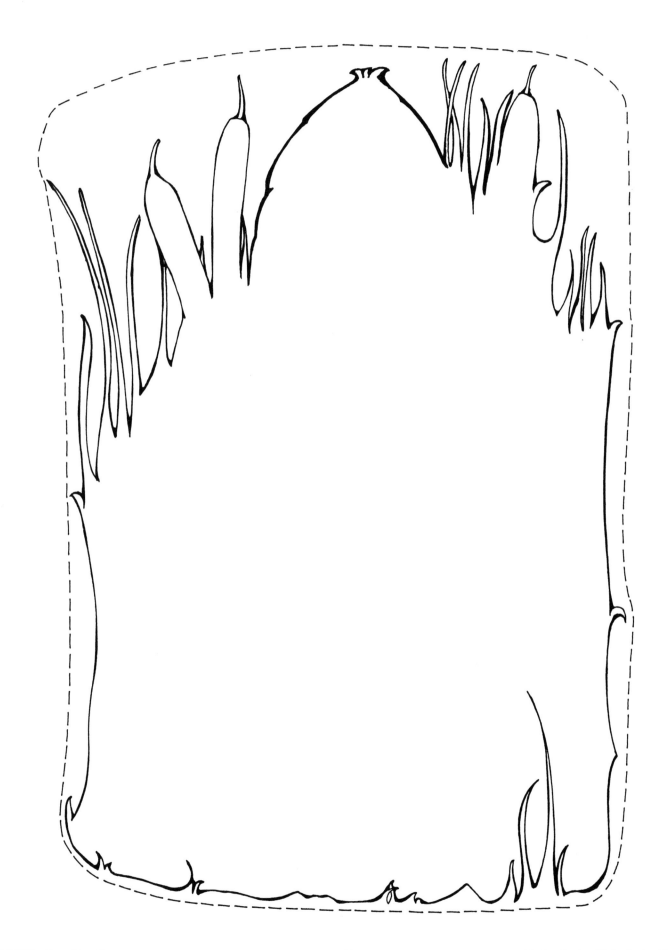

Note: Reproduce this page to use for written stories.

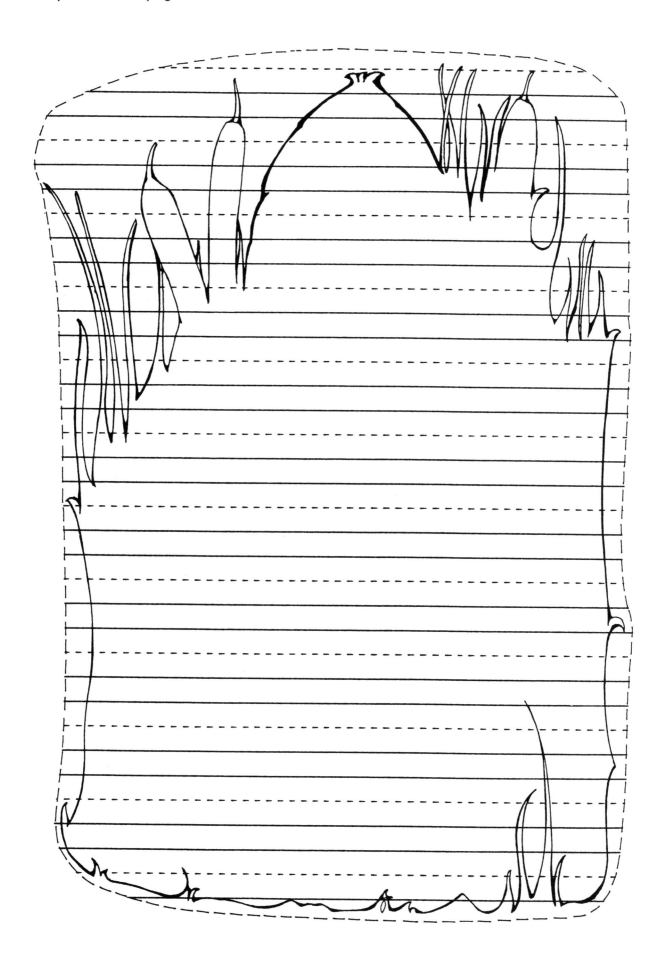

Note: Follow the directions on page 39 for using this page. You can use the duck cover and the duckling patterns to practice the letters of the alphabet. You can make one duck and 26 ducklings (one for each letter). Have the children put the ducklings in a line after the mother duck. Reproduce one duck and one duckling for each letter you are practicing. Make a capital letter on the duck and a lower case letter on each duckling. Mix them up and have children match the correct lower case duckling to the upper case duck.

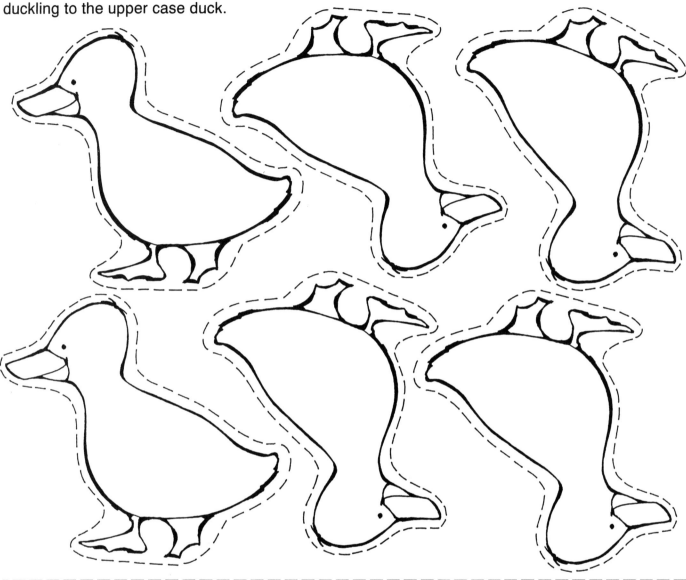

See the big duck.
She is _____.

She is _____.

Her ducklings are _____.

Pet Animal Cage

Read

Guinea Pigs Don't Read Books by Colleen Bare; Dodd, 1985

Pet Show! by Ezra Jack Keats; Macmillan, 1972

Beetles by Barrie Watts; Franklin Watts, 1989 (Minibeast Series)

Get Ready

1. Bring in one or more pets in a cage (hamster, guinea pig, mouse, rat). Name the animal, the parts of the cage and the equipment needed for the pet. Discuss the best way to care for the pet to keep it healthy and happy.

2. Brainstorm to list all of the kinds of pets you might keep in a cage. See how many books you can locate in your school library to supplement this discussion.

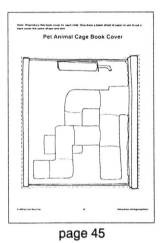
page 45

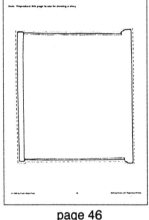
page 46

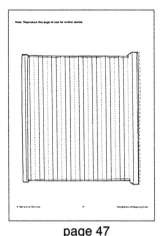
page 47

page 48

Make Individual Books
Prepare story forms and covers. (See page 2.)

1. Draw	2. Complete the Sentence	3. Lines Form
Help children come up with their own topics for stories or use these. Little Pets Child draws a different pet on each cage form and writes or dictates something about each pet. __(kind of pet)__ Child draws the pet in action and writes about it.	Child completes these sentences to create a three-page story. I have a pet _____. It eats _____. It plays _____.	Children write their own stories about pets that live in small cages. Possible story starters are... My Pet Pet Care The Day My Pet Escaped The _____ Family

Make a Group Book
Reproduce the blank form and the animals on page 48.

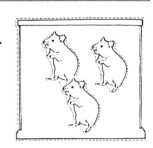

Give each child a blank form. They may choose one of the animals from page 48 to paste to the blank form or draw one of their own. They color the animal in an interesting way. Then they dictate or write a descriptive phrase using at least two describing words ("a fat, fluffy hamster," "a black, furry bunny," "my brown and white mouse with a long scaly tail").

Making Books with Beginning Writers

Note: Reproduce this book cover for each child. Give them a blank sheet of paper to use to cut a back cover the same shape and size.

Pet Animal Cage Book Cover

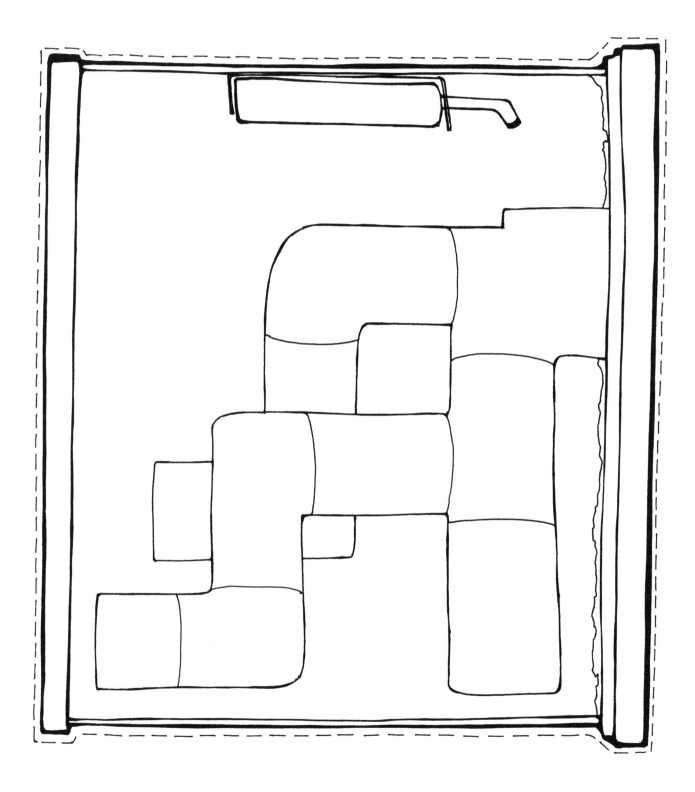

Note: Reproduce this page to use for drawing a story.

Note: Reproduce this page to use for written stories.

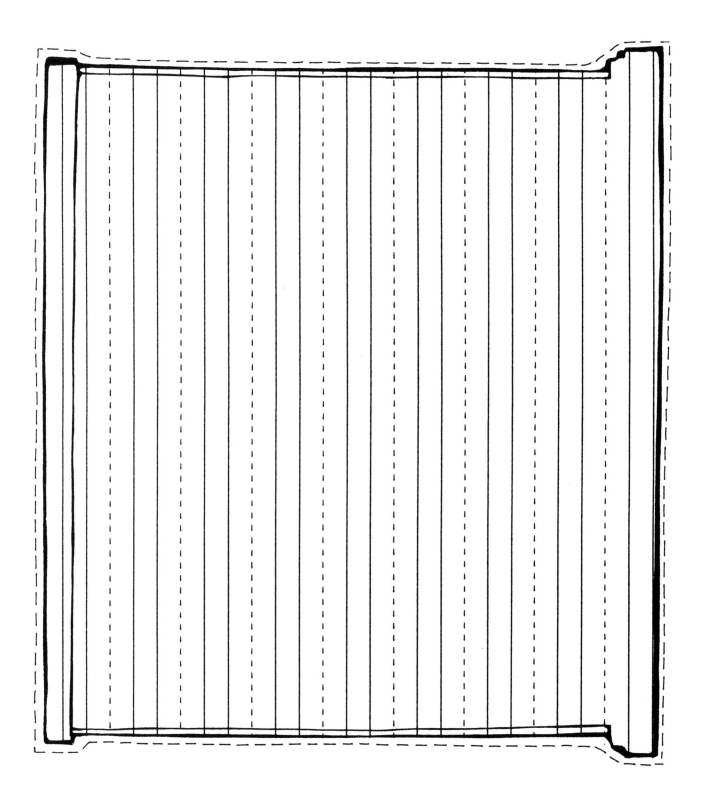

Note: Follow the directions on page 44 for using this page. You can use these animals for patterning activities. Reproduce the animals in different colors and in different sizes. Lay out a pattern and have your students try to copy it. Start with simple ABABAB patterns and work up to more complicated ones.

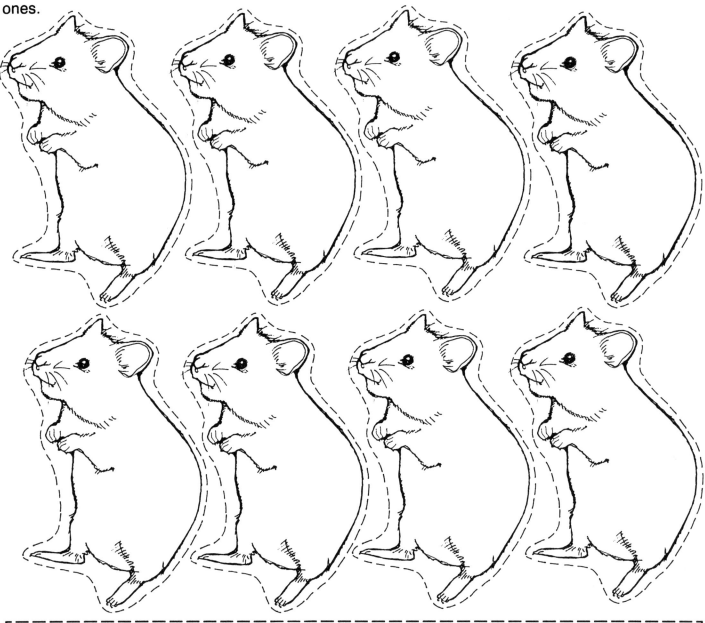

I have a pet _____.

It eats _____.

It plays _____.